Start Investing Now

Build Your Investment Portfolio
for $5 per month

by

Craig L. Israelsen, Ph.D.

Designer of the *7Twelve*® Portfolio

www.7TwelvePortfolio.com

Publication date
May 2018

Price in $US: $7.12

Introduction

This is a "***why-to***" and "***how-to***" book about investing—for normal people on a normal budget.

It's a short book because you may not really dig all the nuances of investing, but you recognize that you need to do it. I get it. For the technical geeks like me, you may also enjoy Appendix A, B, and C.

It's also important to talk about several behavioral aspects of investing that separate successful investors from frenetic investors, so a bit of time will be spent on the "why" of the "how". Turns out that investing is an effective teacher of life lessons...if we do it thoughtfully.

Investing is about money, and money is a magnifier. Money magnifies virtues, as well as vices. Handle it with care. If money turns you inward to focus on only yourself, you will be at risk. If it turns you outward to others, you can be the source of much good.

Quick overview of this book:

Section 1: Why Start Investing Early in Life?

Section 2: The Characteristics of Successful Investors

Section 3: What Should I Invest My Money In?

Section 4   How Much Should I Invest? And How Often?

Section 5: How Do I Measure the Performance of My Investments?

Section 6: How Long Should I Invest?

Section 7: How Much Do I Need to Have in My Investment Accounts When I Retire?

Section 8: I Will Eventually Take Money out of My Investments--How Does That Work?

Technical Appendix A: Will I Run Out of Money?
Technical Appendix B: Are You a Reluctant Investor?
Technical Appendix C: Introduction to the *7Twelve*® Portfolio

If you're in a hurry, there is a **Master Summary** on the next page...

Master Summary

- Start investing now. Simply do your best. Set a goal to **save 10-15% of your annual income** into a diversified portfolio of investments. Do that for 30-40 years—and you'll be set!

- If you can commit at least $5 per month, invest in the **Homestead Value Fund.** Use the Automatic Investing Program (AIP) at Homestead Funds—otherwise, the minimum initial investment is $500. Click on the link below to open an application form; section 6 is where you will sign up for the **Automatic Investing Program**. If you have questions call Homestead Funds at 800-258-3030.

  https://www.homesteadfunds.com/wp-content/uploads/IndividualORJoint-Account-App.pdf

- If you have $1,000 to invest, open an account at Vanguard and start with the **Vanguard STAR mutual fund**. It's a *fund-of-funds* that invests in 11 other Vanguard mutual funds—meaning that you will have broad diversification inside of just one fund. Click on the link below to learn more. Need help getting started? Call Vanguard at 877-320-3099. Just tell them you want to open an account in the STAR fund. The representative will guide you through the process.

  https://personal.vanguard.com/us/funds/snapshot?FundId=0056&FundIntExt=INT&funds_disable_redirect=true

- After you open a mutual fund account at Homestead or Vanguard, make a commitment to **invest additional money each month**. If you choose the AIP at Homestead, that will already be happening. If you decide to invest in the Vanguard STAR fund you will also want to establish an automatic monthly investment with Vanguard.

- After you start investing, don't expect overnight success. **Investing is like a crockpot, not a microwave**. It takes time. As in, 15 to 20 years. Don't be a helicopter investor (you know, the one that hovers over their portfolio, freaking out over every hiccup).

- When you retire, if you only **withdraw 4% of your portfolio's account balance at the end of each year**, your money will likely last for at least 40 more years. (Whether 4% of the balance is enough to live on is a different matter. More on this topic in *Technical Appendix A*.)

- **Remember why** you are doing this:
    - to be a wise steward of your resources and to prepare for future needs and goals.
    - to "grow" your talents and abilities by setting financial goals and sticking to them.

- After you have chosen your mutual fund(s) and have initiated the automatic investing program, **turn your attention to more important parts of your life**. Care for the physical, emotional, social, and spiritual needs of yourself and those around you. Focus outward. Money is a means to achieve goals, not an end in itself. Use financial resources to facilitate life experiences with others as well as meaningful service opportunities. Memories last far longer than things.

- Finally: **teach someone** else what you have learned about investing.

Section 1

Why Start Investing Early in Life?

This issue is quite straightforward. Sooner is better than later—particularly if we're talking about saving for retirement. There is a bunch of fancy math that proves all this, but I think the table below will pretty much nail it for you.

If you start saving (i.e., investing) 8% of your annual income each year at the age of 25 (assuming you are earning $35,000 and that your income increases by 3% each year), you'll have a bit over $1 million in your retirement investment portfolio (assuming you earned an 8% investment return each year). That is a great achievement. But even if you can only save 3 or 4% of your income right now, great! Simply do your best at every age. Don't be discouraged...because that won't help.

If you wait until you're 35 to start investing, your final balance at age 65 falls to about $574,000. And it gets worse from there. Obviously, if you invest more of your income combined with a higher portfolio rate of return, your final account value increases. But did you notice that the final portfolio value at age 65 goes up in a disproportionate way? This is actually a really good thing! Here is the explanation...

If your annual savings rate goes from 8% to 10%, that is a **25% increase**. Likewise, if your investment portfolio return goes from 8% to 10%, that is also a **25% increase**. But, your account value at age 65 goes up **by more than 100%** (from $1,033,899 to $2,099,861), assuming you started investing at age 25. Even if you start your investment portfolio later in life, there is still a great benefit by investing more each year.

In fact, if you're already over the age of 45, your annual investments (the amount you contribute to your investment account each year) can have a greater impact on your ending portfolio balance than attempting to earn a higher portfolio return. So, rather than increasing the risk of your portfolio in hopes of getting a higher return—simply invest more money into your portfolio if possible. Do more of the heavy lifting yourself, and don't expect the portfolio to be the hero. You can be a hero, too.

Starting Investing at...	Retirement Portfolio Value at Age 65 (Assuming 3% increase in annual income)		
	8% Savings Rate 8% Portfolio Return	10% Savings Rate 10% Portfolio Return	12% Savings Rate 12% Portfolio Return
Age 25 $35,000 Annual Income	1,033,899	2,099,861	4,190,150
Age 35 $47,037 Annual Income	574,635	1,009,425	1,726,741
Age 45 $63,214 Annual Income	288,745	444,429	660,811
Age 55 $84,954 Annual Income	110,781	151,683	199,578

Section 2

The Characteristics of Successful Investors

First characteristic: Successful investors have <u>reasonable expectations</u>.

Your investment portfolio will not have "above average" returns each and every year. Be reasonable! This isn't a fantasy island where all the children are above average. The average return of a diversified 7-asset equally-weighted portfolio that included equities (stocks), bonds, real estate, commodities, and cash was **9.84%** over the past 48 years. (See pie chart to the left for a visual of what a 7-asset portfolio looks like.)

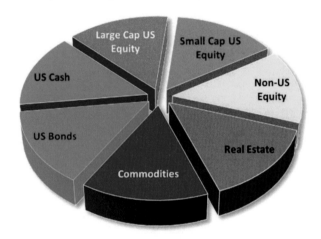

7-Asset Portfolio
Equally Weighted at 14.3% per Asset Class

Between 1970 and 2017, there were some really good years when the performance of the diversified portfolio was above 20% (such as in 1975, 1976, 1980, 1983, 1985, and 2003). In such "good" years, successful investors don't crank up their performance expectations of the portfolio—somehow believing that it's going to pump out 20-plus percent returns year after year.

Likewise, over the past 48 years there have been some discouraging years with negative returns (such as -5.38% in 1974, -3.41% in 1990, -5.51% in 2001, -1.57% in 2002, and -27.61% in 2008---ouch!). But successful investors also don't suddenly lose faith in the portfolio because it stubs its toe a few times.

If your investment portfolio design is based on long-term performance expectations, you have to give it sufficient time to show its stuff. A reasonable way to measure the performance of a diversified portfolio is over 10-year periods. For example, from 1970 to 2017 there were 39 rolling 10-year time periods. The diversified 7-asset portfolio shown above **never experienced a negative 10-year return** (that is, a loss in portfolio value in any of the rolling 10-year periods). In fact, the average 10-year rolling return was 10.33%. Successful investors understand that "long-term investing" is measured in years, not months. And it is most certainly <u>not</u> measured on a daily basis—so don't check your account that often.

Second characteristic: Successful investors <u>discipline themselves</u> by making adequate contributions into their investment portfolio.

Successful investors recognize that a well-designed retirement portfolio has to be adequately fed. Set a goal to invest 10-15% of your annual income. But, if you can only save 4% right now—do that. Focus on what you can do--and then try to consistently do it! I have found that I feel genuine satisfaction if I know I'm doing my best, even if I may not yet be achieving the "ideal goal".

Third characteristic: Successful investors <u>diversify and then measure investment success correctly</u>.

Building a diversified portfolio is like making salsa—we blend a variety of different ingredients together. And, just like it is with salsa, the **result is greater than the sum of the parts**! After building a diversified portfolio, successful investors measure it correctly.

Some investors may be tempted to compare their diversified portfolio against the S&P 500 Index – but that is nonsense. The S&P 500 is not a diversified portfolio, but rather a collection of stocks of the 500 largest US companies. It contains no bonds, no real estate, no commodities, and no foreign (non-US) stock. Think of it like this: the S&P 500 represents 500 different varieties of tomatoes, whereas a diversified, multi-asset portfolio represents actual salsa! Your portfolio needs to BE *investment salsa*.

Fourth characteristic: Successful investors <u>lead balanced lives</u>.

This statement does not imply that successful investors don't face challenges in their lives—they most certainly do. But, successful investors tend to focus on things that are going well, rather than things that are not. They focus on progress, rather than distance from the goal. In short, successful investors have a balanced perspective on life that acknowledges challenges and struggles, but with an overriding spirit of optimism and courage. Everyone needs a friend, and your first friend should be yourself. Set high goals, but be reasonable regarding how long it may take to achieve them.

Successful investors not only have diversified portfolios, but they also have diversified lives. This type of life balance provides the needed anchors when one aspect of life takes a severe blow. Physical, emotional, social, and spiritual balance are all needed. Without life balance, small issues are often blown out of proportion into big issues, distracting us from the things we *can* control. Even worse, things that are "non-issues" can become major obstacles without a balanced perspective. Successful investors recognize that wealth is not the end goal, but a means to accomplish one's life goals and aspirations. Gratitude is a common characteristic of people leading balanced lives.

Finally, the word "balance" does not necessarily imply "equal". For example, an orchestra has far more violins than oboes, but the desired musical sound is "balanced". Seek *harmonic* balance in life, rather than assuming that everything needs to be *arithmetically* balanced.

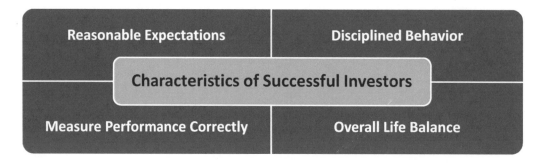

Section 3

What Should I Invest My Money In?

The best place to start as a new investor is with a **mutual fund**. Many people invest their money in mutual funds to prepare for retirement. A mutual fund is a portfolio (collection) of stocks, bonds, real estate, etc. There are literally thousands of mutual funds to choose from—which is both a blessing and a curse. Having so many choices can lead to "paralysis by analysis". This book was written to help you avoid that.

Ideally, an investor needs a handful or two of different mutual funds to be "diversified". Diversification helps reduce the risk of loss and also reduces volatility of your portfolio's performance. However, if you can only start one mutual fund right now—do that. Again, the most important issue is starting, rather than waiting until you can do it "perfectly". Children start to talk long before they can do it fluently...and begin walking long before they can run.

Which mutual fund you invest in is largely determined by what you can afford right now. So, I've put together a list of mutual funds that can be started for as little as $5 per month. On the next page there is a list of **broadly diversified** mutual funds that can be started for $1,000 or less.

Homestead Funds

Homestead is a mutual fund company in Virginia. Their website is http://homesteadfunds.com. Their phone number is 1-800-258-3030. They have several different mutual funds. Below are four of their funds that can be utilized to build the starting foundation of a "diversified" investment portfolio, along with their average yearly return over the past 15 years and how often that type of fund has a positive return (one way to measure "risk"). Each of these funds invests in a specific asset class (such as bonds, or stocks from small US companies, or stocks from large US companies, etc.). To have a diversified portfolio you will need to invest in several different Homestead funds.

Name of Homestead Mutual Fund (and Fund Symbol)	This mutual fund invests in...	15-Year Average Annualized Return of this Actual Fund (2003-2017)	Percentage of time this type of mutual fund loses money during a calendar year over the past 48 years (1970-2017)
Homestead Value (HOVLX)	Large US Stocks	10.19%	19% of the time
Homestead Small Company Stock (HSCSX)	Small US Stocks	12.11%	29% of the time
Homestead Short-Term Bond (HOSBX)	US Bonds	3.05%	6% of the time
Homestead International Equity (HISIX)	Non-US Stocks	7.75%	29% of the time

As you examine the Homestead mutual funds in the table above, don't make the mistake of simply picking the fund with the highest return over the past 15 years (HSCSX) or the lowest volatility (HOSBX). Performance ebbs and flows among mutual funds that invest in different things, so it's smart to assemble a diverse variety of mutual funds. Choose several of the Homestead mutual funds to create your salsa-like investment portfolio.

With their automatic investing plan, Homestead waives the normal initial investment of $500. You can literally build an investment portfolio using the four mutual funds shown above for $20 per month ($5 each month into each fund) if you automate the monthly investment. (An automatic monthly investment is a free service where you authorize Homestead to electronically withdraw your monthly investment from your checking or savings account.) Of course, you can invest more than the $5 monthly minimum, so you should arrange to have them withdraw as much as is feasible each month or year.

WHAT type of investment account should I set up?

There are two basic types of investment accounts: *regular investment account* and *individual retirement account* (IRA). Regular investment accounts have fewer rules than IRA accounts, but IRA accounts offer tax protection. There are two types of IRA accounts: the traditional IRA (save on taxes now) and the Roth IRA (save on taxes in retirement). Remember, you are investing money in mutual funds—but you still have to choose whether to establish a regular account or an IRA account. For most people with modest incomes, the Roth IRA is generally the most useful. If married, it's best to set up separate IRA accounts to maximize the amount each person can invest each year.

Vanguard provides an excellent review of the various types of investment accounts that you can set up. Click on this link: https://investor.vanguard.com/investing/investment-accounts

IMPORTANT: There is a $15 yearly account maintenance fee at Homestead for setting up an IRA account, so if you plan to invest a small amount of money you may want to only invest in one Homestead mutual fund rather than four (so that you don't duplicate the $15 annual fee). Regular (non-IRA) investment accounts at Homestead don't charge the $15 annual account maintenance fee.

Diversified Mutual Funds (One-Stop Shopping)

If you have a bit more money to invest you may want to consider mutual funds that are already diversified across several asset classes (meaning not just US stocks, but a variety of "asset classes" such as US stocks, non-US stocks, bonds, real estate, etc.). The funds in the table below are broadly diversified mutual funds...kind of like investing in a Swiss army knife.

Broadly Diversified Mutual Funds	Symbol	Initial Purchase Requirement	Subsequent Investment Minimum	Annual Account Fee	Annual Expense Ratio (lower is better)	15-Year Average Annualized Return (2003-2017)
Schwab MarketTrack Growth	SWHGX	$100	$1	None	0.52%	8.20%
Schwab MarketTrack Balanced	SWBGX	$100	$1	None	0.50%	6.93%
Vanguard STAR	VGSTX	$1,000	$1	$20 if account is under $10,000. $20 fee waived if you sign up for electronic document delivery	0.32%	8.37%
Pax Balanced Fund (Investor share class)	PAXWX	$1,000	$50	None	0.93%	6.61%

Schwab phone and website: 877-310-7739
https://www.schwab.com/public/schwab/investing/accounts_products/investment/mutual_funds/mutual_fund_portfolio/market_track_portfolios

Vanguard phone and website: 877-320-3099
https://personal.vanguard.com/us/funds/snapshot?FundId=0056&FundIntExt=INT&funds_disable_redirect=true

Pax World Funds phone and website: 800-372-7827
https://paxworld.com/funds/pax-balanced-fund/

Vanguard STAR would be my suggestion if you have $1,000 available to open a mutual fund account. Vanguard is a *fund-of-funds*. It is a fund that invests in 11 other Vanguard mutual funds and ends up with an overall composition of roughly 60% in stock (both US and non-US), 25% in bonds, and the remainder in short-term reserves (like cash). The result is broad, multi-asset diversification—salsa, in other words. If your account balance is under $10,000 Vanguard will charge a $20 per year account maintenance fee. However, if you enroll in "electronic delivery of documents" (meaning you receive information from Vanguard via email rather than paper mail) the $20 account maintenance fee is waived. So, sign up! Also consider setting up automatic monthly investments with Vanguard so that you continue to add money to Vanguard STAR each month.

The Schwab MarketTrack funds ("Growth" and "Balanced") are also two excellent mutual funds to begin if you don't have the $1,000 that is required for the initial investment at Vanguard. These two Schwab mutual funds can be started for $100 each. But, you can also initially invest more if you wish. $100 is simply the minimum initial investment. Pax Balanced Investor is an SRI fund. SRI represents "socially responsible investing". Pax actually describes their investing approach as "ESG" -- which stands for Environmental, Social and Governance. According to PAX, "ESG factors offer portfolio managers added insight into the quality of a company's management, culture, risk profile and other characteristics." For investors that wish to invest in accordance with certain social and environmental mandates PAXWX will be a fine choice. However, it should be noted that PAXWX under-performed Vanguard STAR over the past 15 years.

Mutual Fund Costs

All mutual funds have a cost that the investor pays for. That cost is called the "annual expense ratio". An important goal is to keep the cost as low as possible—but it is not the only goal. Vanguard is famous for keeping costs low. The Vanguard STAR fund has an expense ratio of 0.32%. That means you will pay 32 cents per year for every $100 you have invested in the fund. That is a low expense ratio by industry standards. The average mutual fund expense ratio is 1.07% (based on thousands of mutual funds). Thus, the Vanguard STAR fund is 1/3 the cost of the average fund.

The two Schwab funds also have much lower-than-average expense ratios. The mutual funds at Homestead have below average expense ratios. Homestead Value has an expense ratio of 0.62%, and the Homestead Small Company Stock fund's expense ratio is 0.89%. The Homestead International Equity expense ratio is 0.99% and the Homestead Short-Term Bond Fund is 0.76%.

Generally speaking, mutual funds that invest overseas have higher expense ratios. Another cost that some mutual funds have is a "load", or sales commission when you invest money and/or take money out of your mutual fund. None of the funds discussed in this book charge a sales commission, and as a result, are referred to as "no-load" funds.

Section 4

How Much Should I Invest? And How Often?

The simple answer is that you should invest as much, and as often, as you feasibly can. Generally speaking, to have enough saved for retirement you will need to save 10-15% of your monthly or annual income (as discussed in Section 1) throughout your 30-to-40-year working career. If you're a late starter, don't freak out. Just do your best going forward. If you're over 45, saving more each year will have more impact on your ending balance than attempting to crank up the performance of your portfolio, because that also cranks up the risk of losses in your portfolio.

For many people, the most logical investing frequency is monthly—and it's best if you set it up so that your investments automatically happen. Let the mutual fund company withdraw the money from your checking or savings account so that you don't have to think about it.

Let's consider a hypothetical example of someone who opened an account in the Vanguard STAR fund on January 1, 2003 with $1,000. Then, starting in February of 2003, they automatically invested $100 into the fund for the next 15 years, through December of 2017. As shown below, their consistent investing behavior rewarded them with an ending balance of over $37,000. Notice the steady upward climb of the account balance in the mutual fund over time—that is what happens when you consistently invest during good times and bad. Don't worry about how the "market" is doing—just keep investing. In fact, invest a bit extra when your mutual fund has experienced a negative return (something that doesn't happen very often in the Vanguard STAR fund).

In this example, the total out-of-pocket investment was $18,900—the rest was the growth of the mutual fund. As you can see from the table on page 8, Vanguard STAR had a 15-year annualized return of just under 8.4% from January of 2003 to December of 2017.

An average return of 8% is achievable if you will be consistent in your investing. Plus, consistent monthly investments help reduce the volatility in your investment account balance (as shown below in the graph). No wild swings, but rather a steady upward trend. Investing is like climbing a mountain: just keep consistently moving forward—don't worry about beating "the market".

Account Balance Growth of Vanguard STAR Mutual Fund
15-Years from 2003-2017

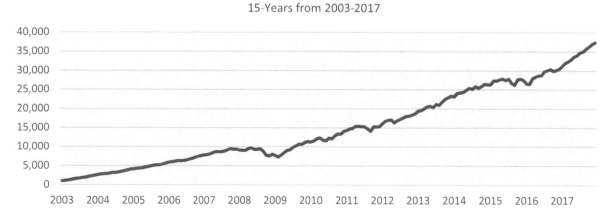

Section 5

How Do I Measure the Performance of My Investments?

The performance of mutual funds can be measured daily, weekly, monthly, annually, and over multiple-year periods. For example, below is a summary of the performance of the Vanguard STAR fund as of April 30, 2018. As shown below, the Vanguard STAR fund had a one-day return of -0.34% on April 30, 2018. But, over the prior 15 years it had an average return each year of 8.07%. (But keep in mind that this is an *average*. The return was NOT 8.07% each and every year).

1-Day	-0.34%	Less useful time period
1-Week	-0.41%	
1-Month	-0.07%	
3-Month	-3.68%	
1-Year	10.60%	
3-Years	6.67%	More useful time period
5-Years	8.15%	
10-Years	6.95%	
15-Years	8.07%	

Short-term performance measurements (the ones in the red box) are nearly useless. It's just noise. Checking the performance of a diversified mutual fund each day would be like planting an oak tree and checking its growth every 24 hours. Hey, it's an oak tree. It grows S L O W L Y. It's the same with an investment—you have to be patient and give it time. Remember: crockpot, not microwave.

But, if you must check…performance over 3, 5, 10, or 15 years (the numbers in blue) is far more useful and indicative of what you can expect over the "long haul". You can find the performance of mutual funds on www.Morningstar.com by entering the mutual fund symbol. (In the case of Vanguard STAR, the symbol is VGSTX.) Every mutual fund has a unique symbol (or identifier).

The key is to **not** become a "helicopter investor". Don't hover and obsess over your investments. Check them every now and then, perhaps every 3 months or so. But consider the advice of a mutual fund manager: "***If you want to take volatility out of your portfolio, check it less often!***"

The most important performance measure of your investments is if you are making timely progress toward your goals and objectives. It doesn't matter if you're "beating the market" or not. Besides, what is "the market"? There is a US cash market, a US bond market, many non-US bond markets, a US stock market, dozens of non-US stock markets, etc.

Do yourself a favor and **(1)** simply build a diversified portfolio (with several mutual funds from Homestead and/or one of the multi-asset mutual funds listed in section 3), **(2)** invest money each month (or quarter or year), **(3)** check your performance occasionally, and **(4)** refuse to compare your results against recent "hot" performing funds or the ubiquitous S&P 500 Index. Neither the hotshot funds nor the S&P 500 Index have anything to do with your broadly diversified, prudent approach to investing. Investors who get distracted with those types of performance comparisons end up chasing yesterday's winners—not a good approach to long-term investing.

Section 6

How Long Should I Invest?

As long as it takes to reach your goals...or get as close as you can. For retirement, that probably means investing for 30-40 years. To save for a down payment on a home, perhaps 5-10 years. To make the down payment on a vehicle, perhaps it will require 3-5 years. Generally speaking, investing is a "long-run" experience.

So, how long is the "long-run"? How about the last 92 years from 1926 to 2017?!

1926-2017	US Large Stocks	US Small Stocks	US Bonds	US Cash	4-Asset Diversified Portfolio
Average Annualized Return (the higher the better)	10.16%	11.35%	5.30%	3.41%	9.39%
Standard Deviation of Returns (the lower the better)	19.8%	31.3%	5.7%	3.2%	15.1%
Best Year	54%	143%	33%	15%	58%
Worst Year	-43%	-58%	-3%	0%	-30%
Percentage of Years with a Positive Return	73.9%	68.5%	90.2%	97.8%	76.1%

These figures do not account for inflation

Over the past 92 years, an investment in large US stocks produced an average return of 10.16%. But, there was quite a bit of variation in the year-to-year returns, as evidenced by a standard deviation of 19.8% (essentially 2x higher than the average return). The cool part is that the US stock market (large companies) had a positive annual return 73.9% of the time. That's a pretty impressive batting average.

Even more impressive, however, is that a diversified investor that invested in all four asset classes (40% in US large stock, 25% in US small stock, 25% in US bonds, and 10% in cash) had an average return of 9.39%—but with almost 25% less volatility and a more frequent positive annual return than an investor who only invested in large US stocks. It pays to diversify. Remember the "life balance" goal? Diversification creates investment "balance".

Here is the important thing to remember: the longer you invest the more likely you are to experience a positive return. If, starting in 1926, you stayed invested in the four-asset diversified portfolio shown above for at least 5 years, you would have had a positive return 93% of the time. If you stayed invested for at least 10 years, you have a positive return 100% of the time. So, what is the mantra? Stay in the saddle for at least 10 years and you'll very likely have a positive experience. In fact, if you stay invested in a diversified portfolio for at least 35 years you have an 88% chance of having an average return of 9% or higher. Loyalty is a virtue—particularly as it applies to investing.

Section 7

How Much Do I Need to Have in My Investment Accounts When I Retire?

As you might imagine, there is not a single magic number because of the differences among people. So, while it's not possible to state an actual number that applies to everyone, we *can* talk about the amount of money you should have when you retire in comparison to how much you were earning the year before you retired. In other words, it's not about having a set amount—it's about having a certain "multiple" of the amount you were earning before you retired.

For example, let's assume your annual income at the age of 65 is $100,000 and you plan to retire next year at the age of 66. If you have saved up $500,000 in your retirement accounts by the age of 66, you have a "5x Retirement Account Multiple (or "5x RAM")—meaning that your retirement account is 5 times larger than your annual income prior to retirement.

As shown in the table below, if you have a 5x RAM, totaling in $500,000, and you withdraw 4% of that balance, you will have $20,000 for your first year of retirement (plus any other income sources such as social security, etc.). That $20,000 withdrawal from your portfolio represents 20% of your pre-retirement income of $100,000. (This 20% is an example of what is called "income replacement", represented by the right-hand column of the table. Income replacement is the percentage of your pre-retirement income that you withdraw during each year of your retirement.) In other words, if you have a 5x RAM and a 4% withdrawal rate, your income replacement is 20%. The equation is very simple:

RAM * % Withdrawal Rate = % Income Replacement

Retirement Account Multiple of Pre-Retirement Income (RAM)	Multiplied by	Initial Withdrawal Rate (%)	Equals	% of Pre-Retirement Income Being Replaced in First Year of Retirement
3x	*	4%	=	12%
5x	*	4%	=	20%
10x	*	4%	=	40%
12x	*	4%	=	48%
15x	*	4%	=	60%

Of course, withdrawing money from your investments is only one source of retirement income—you may also have other sources. And it's obviously also important to control spending in retirement, just as we need to during our pre-retirement years. But the goal is quite clear: If we assume that you will be withdrawing 4% each year from your retirement accounts, you will need to have a RAM that will allow you to "replace" enough of your pre-retirement income to meet your needs. The larger the RAM, the better off you will be in terms of retirement income.

Set a goal to achieve a 10x or 12x RAM by the year of your retirement. If you start early, and invest 15% of your income, you will likely achieve that goal. It's also really important to have a life plan when you retire. Don't simply stop working—stay active as you move into the next chapter of life.

Section 8

I Will Eventually Take Money out of My Investments--How Does That Work?

Based on your investing objective (saving for a car, a home, your retirement, etc.), you will eventually withdraw money from your investment account. In other words, you will sell some or all of the shares of your mutual fund(s) back to the mutual fund company. When you sell shares, it is a taxable event, unless you set up your mutual funds as Roth IRA accounts (which is a tax-exempt type of account). Vanguard provides an excellent review of the various types of investment accounts that you can set up. Click on this link: https://investor.vanguard.com/investing/investment-accounts

If you have been saving/investing for a down payment on a car or on a home, you will simply sell shares of your mutual fund(s) to withdraw the needed amount of money.

If you have been saving/investing for your retirement, you will withdraw money from your investment accounts each month, each quarter, each year, or whatever frequency you decide. Your retirement accounts will likely be a combination of mutual funds that you started on your own, plus mutual funds in your 401k plan. While not everyone has access to a 401k plan, many do.

During your retirement years, the big question is "how much can I safely withdraw each year from my retirement accounts so that I don't run out of money too soon?" This is a complicated question because there are a lot of variables, but I've boiled it down to one table. The basic question is this: *what percentage of my retirement portfolio can I withdraw and still have a high probability that it will last for at least 35 years before I run out of money?*

Here is the scenario: Let's assume you have $250,000 saved up in your retirement accounts. (You may have more than that, but this gives us a starting point for the analysis. Furthermore, the amount of money being analyzed is less important than the "Success Ratio" statistics in the table on the next page).

If you're a conservative investor, you might have an overall "asset allocation" (or portfolio design) that is less risky by having 25% of your money invested in stock-based mutual funds and 75% in mutual funds that invest in bonds and cash. Or, if you're bold, your retirement portfolio may have a 65% allocation to stock mutual funds and 35% allocated to bond and money market (i.e., cash) mutual funds. These are simply two examples of the possible "asset allocation" of your portfolio.

As shown in the table on the next page, if you had a conservative 25% stocks/75% bonds and cash retirement portfolio, withdrew 4% of your portfolio balance in the first year of retirement, and then increased the amount of the annual withdrawal by 3% each year (which is referred to as a *cost of living adjustment* or COLA), your portfolio would have survived in 93% of the rolling 35-year periods between 1926 and 2017. In other words, 93% of the time, your portfolio would have stayed intact for a period of at least 35 years. On the other hand, a growth-oriented 65/35 portfolio had a 98% success ratio of lasting at least 35 years before it was out of money. Assuming a retirement period beginning at age 65 and ending at 100, the average ending balance at age 100 was $1.1 million for the 25/75 portfolio and roughly $4 million for the 65/35 portfolio—a big difference.

Retirement Portfolio Survival Summary
$250,000 starting balance (as an example)

Success Ratio = Percentage of Time the Retirement Portfolio Survived for at Least 35 Years
Retirement at age 65

58 Rolling 35-Year Periods between 1926-2017	3% Initial Withdrawal Rate 3% Cost of Living Adjustment Total of all annual withdrawals = $453,466		4% Initial Withdrawal Rate 3% Cost of Living Adjustment Total of all annual withdrawals = $604,621		5% Initial Withdrawal Rate 3% Cost of Living Adjustment Total of all annual withdrawals = $755,776	
	Conservative 25 / 75 Portfolio	Growth 65 / 35 Portfolio	Conservative 25 / 75 Portfolio	Growth 65 / 35 Portfolio	Conservative 25 / 75 Portfolio	Growth 65 / 35 Portfolio
Success Ratio*	100%	100%	93%	98%	60%	91%
Average Balance at Age 100	$1,752,048	$5,068,173	$1,145,850	$4,039,937	$628,489	$3,042,577

25/75 Portfolio: 15% Large Cap US Stock, 10% Small Cap US Stock, 55% US Bonds, 20% Cash
65/35 Portfolio: 40% Large Cap US Stock, 25% Small Cap US Stock, 25% US Bonds, 10% Cash

* The success ratio will be the same regardless of the starting balance of the retirement portfolio.
The average balance at age 100 will differ if you assume a different starting account balance.

If, however, you only need to withdraw 3% of your portfolio balance, with a subsequent 3% annual COLA, either portfolio (25/75 or 65/35) had a 100% success rate of lasting at least 35 years before it was out of money. Assuming you retire at age 65, a portfolio that lasts for at least 35 years takes you to age 100. Many of us will not likely live beyond age 100.

For a retiree that needs to withdraw 5% of the portfolio balance in the first year of their retirement (in this case, $12,500 assuming a $250,000 starting portfolio balance) and then escalates the withdrawal by 3% each year (meaning $12,875 in year 2, $13,261 in year 3, and so on) the success rate was only 60% for the conservative retirement portfolio and 91% for the growth retirement portfolio.

The message is quite clear: If you plan on withdrawing 5% or more of your retirement portfolio, combined with a 3% COLA, you will need to build a more growth-oriented retirement portfolio, one that is roughly 65% stock mutual funds and 35% bond mutual funds and cash. This approach means your annual withdrawal from your retirement portfolio will never decrease, even if the portfolio had a bad year, because the COLA forces the amount you withdraw each year to increase. While this is probably what a lot of people want – a steadily increasing retirement income – it puts a lot of pressure on the investment portfolio, particularly in years when it doesn't perform well.

Another approach is to simply withdraw 4% of the portfolio's ending balance each year and not worry about a COLA. For example, if your retirement account balance was $250,000 at the end of the year 2020, and you decided to withdraw 4% of the balance, you would sell $10,000 worth of your mutual fund shares: $250,000 * .04 = $10,000. That $10,000 would then form part or all of your income for the year 2021. This approach means that after a bad year (like 2008), the withdrawal from your investment portfolio will likely be reduced because your portfolio balance went down. In other words, there will be some years during retirement in which you will have to take a pay-cut because your portfolio won't always perform well.

While a retirement income "pay-cut" some years may be tough, this approach does guarantee that your portfolio will not run out of money for at least 40 years. In fact, assuming you build a 65/35 growth-oriented retirement portfolio, your ending balance after 40 years will likely be over $1 million (assuming a starting balance of $250,00 in the first year of your retirement) if you only **withdraw 4% of your portfolio's _ending account balance_ each year**. Again, that may mean your annual withdrawal is reduced in some years. That's the tradeoff—guaranteed retirement portfolio survival for at least 40 years BUT a high likelihood that your annual income during retirement will go down during some years.

Key points to remember and put into practice:

1) Save/invest 10% to 15% of your income each year, starting as soon as possible.

2) Invest in diversified, multi-asset mutual funds, such as the Vanguard STAR mutual fund. Or, build your own diversified portfolio of mutual funds (see Technical Appendix C—An Introduction to the *7Twelve*® Portfolio).

3) Keep investing regardless of what the "market" is doing. If the US stock market is doing well, great. If the market is going down, great. When the US stock market or stock markets around the world are going down, invest a little extra in those years. The key to investing is to BUY LOW, BE PATIENT, SELL HIGH. You do that by investing more money during the "bad" years. This particular behavior is what separates successful investors from unsuccessful investors.

4) If you invest in several different mutual funds, rebalance them annually or every other year. That simply means that you add more money to the mutual funds that are lagging behind at the end of each year. If you invest in a single diversified fund (such as Vanguard STAR) it will be rebalanced automatically for you.

5) Remember that money is a magnifier. Let it magnify your virtues, not your vices.

6) Once you have your investment habits established, focus on more important things. Don't react to the market noise of each day. Investing is a long-term, multi-decade endeavor.

7) Enjoy the ride. **Count your blessings more often than you count your money**.

Questions or comments? Email me at craig@7TwelvePortfolio.com

Performance of investment products, such as mutual funds, is variable—be patient.
Losses can occur in the short run.
This book talks about mutual funds, but does not guarantee their performance.

Technical Appendix A

Will I Run Out of Money?
By Craig L. Israelsen

Reprinted by permission from *Financial Planning Magazine*
https://www.financial-planning.com/news/pension-like-retirement-income-in-a-401-k-world-with-rmds

It's doubtful there is a more compelling question. Every retiree will likely ask this question at some point.

This section attempts to simplify the very complicated issue of retirement portfolio durability—understanding very clearly that as we simplify we necessarily ignore some important variables, such as taxation, differences among people in their retirement spending, etc.

Let's start with a benchmark of retirement income that has largely disappeared: the defined benefit pension. The hallmark characteristic of this source of retirement income was that it was a fixed amount each month for the rest of the retiree's life. Typically, the monthly income would never increase. The certainty of this approach was reassuring regardless if the fixed amount each month was sufficient to meet the retiree's spending needs. Simply knowing the amount of the monthly pension check was highly valued. The retiree had no idea what rate of return the pension fund was earning—that was not their issue, but rather the responsibility of the former employer. Fast forward to today...we live in a defined contribution world where each person is essentially their own pension-fund manager.

Is it possible to re-create a defined benefit monthly retirement income in a defined contribution world? Yes, of course. But, there are tradeoffs.

As shown in Table 1, a $500,000 retirement portfolio is invested in an account that has a fixed annual return of 2% (say, in laddered CD's). If the retiree withdraws 5% of the starting balance the fixed annual withdrawal would be $25,000. Thus, the retiree knows with certainty the annual return of their retirement portfolio (2%) and the amount they can withdraw annually ($25,000). In this case, the portfolio will last for 25 years before the bucket is empty. End of story.

If, however, the retiree only withdraws $20,000 each year (representing a 4% withdrawal rate) their retirement account that is earning 2% annually will last for 35 years. Finally, if a 3% withdrawal rate is chosen ($15,000 annual withdrawal) the portfolio will last for over 40 years (remaining balance of roughly $198,000 at the end of year 40). It's important to note that the annual withdrawal in each scenario does not increase, meaning there is no annual inflation adjustment. If certainty is the goal, the retiree simply needs to lock in a 2% return and the portfolio slowly erodes right on schedule. The tradeoff in this approach is that the portfolio is completely liquidated at the end of 35 years (assuming a 4% withdrawal rate). There is nothing left if the retiree happens to live longer than 35 years—hence the question "will I run out of money?" The world of certainty presents a problem if the retiree lives an unusually long life.

One solution to this "problem of longevity" is to depart from, at least partially, the "world of certainty". That can happen in at least two ways: the ***annual withdrawal is variable*** and/or the ***return of the portfolio is variable***. To explore this world of semi-certainty I have prepared a chart of retirement portfolio outcomes that you might liken to the laminated play chart that a football coach holds as he paces the sidelines (see Table 2). Let's turn our attention now to the chart. I'll walk you through it.

Table 1. Retirement Income Scenarios
Guaranteed Retirement Income for 25, 35, or 40+ Years with little or no money remaining
Fixed annual withdrawals from a **$500,000 retirement portfolio** with a **2% fixed investment return**

# of Years Retirement Portfolio Remained Solvent	End-of-Year Portfolio Balance Fixed annual withdrawal of $25,000 (5% of starting balance)	End-of-Year Portfolio Balance Fixed annual withdrawal of $20,000 (4% of starting balance)	End-of-Year Portfolio Balance Fixed annual withdrawal of $15,000 (3% of starting balance)
1	$485,000	$490,000	$495,000
2	$469,700	$479,800	$489,900
3	$454,094	$469,396	$484,698
4	$438,176	$458,784	$479,392
5	$421,939	$447,960	$473,980
6	$405,378	$436,919	$468,459
7	$388,486	$425,657	$462,829
8	$371,255	$414,170	$457,085
9	$353,681	$402,454	$451,227
10	$335,754	$390,503	$445,251
11	$317,469	$378,313	$439,156
12	$298,819	$365,879	$432,940
13	$279,795	$353,197	$426,598
14	$260,391	$340,261	$420,130
15	$240,599	$327,066	$413,533
16	$220,411	$313,607	$406,804
17	$199,819	$299,879	$399,940
18	$178,815	$285,877	$392,938
19	$157,392	$271,594	$385,797
20	$135,539	$257,026	$378,513
21	$113,250	$242,167	$371,083
22	$90,515	$227,010	$363,505
23	$67,326	$211,550	$355,775
24	$43,672	$195,781	$347,891
25	$19,546	$179,697	$339,849
26		$163,291	$331,645
27		$146,557	$323,278
28		$129,488	$314,744
29		$112,078	$306,039
30		$94,319	$297,160
31		$76,206	$288,103
32		$57,730	$278,865
33		$38,884	$269,442
34		$19,662	$259,831
35		$55	$250,028
36			$240,028
37			$229,829
38			$219,425
39			$208,814
40			$197,990

The "Retirement Income Menu" (Table 2) is based on a retirement portfolio that starts with a balance of $500,000. But, you can easily adjust the information in the chart to any other starting balance. For example, if you want to analyze a $1,000,000 retirement portfolio simply multiply all the dollar figures in the chart by 2 (the percentage figures and non-dollar figures remain the same regardless of portfolio size). The analysis assumed a maximum retirement period of 40 years. Finally, inasmuch as the RMD (RMD stands for required minimum distribution) is included in the table the analysis assumes that the retiree begins taking distributions from their retirement portfolio at age 70.5. To learn more about the RMD please click on the link below: https://personal.vanguard.com/us/whatweoffer/accountservices/requiredminimumdistribution

The table is divided into two halves based on the performance of the retirement portfolio: fixed 2% annual return (world of certainty) and a retirement portfolio that has a variable return (world of uncertainty). Let's first examine the world of certainty.

Assuming a fixed annual return of 2%, the retiree has three options regarding how to withdraw money (understanding that the RMD removes that choice if the account is governed by RMD guidelines). The first choice is to simply withdraw a set amount of money each year (see column A). In this analysis, the withdrawal was set to be $20,000 which represents 4% of the starting balance of $500,000. There was no variation in the annual withdrawal meaning that there was no annual cost-of-living-adjustment (COLA). In this scenario, the portfolio lasted for 35 years at which point it was empty (see also the middle data column in Table 1). The total amount withdrawn over 35 years was $700,000 (plus a $55 remaining residue at the end of the 35th year). But, at this point, the portfolio was empty. If the retiree is still alive, they have run out of money. Problem.

An alternative (again, still in the world of certainty of a 2% fixed annual portfolio return) is to annually withdraw 4% of the portfolio's end-of-year value (see column B). As can be seen, this results in slightly less being withdrawn each year ($18,593 average annual withdrawal over the first 10 years vs. fixed $20,000 annual withdrawal), but the tradeoff is that the portfolio lasted for over 40 years as shown by the ending balance of $215,688 at the end of year 40 (last row of table). **A very simple solution to not outliving your retirement portfolio is to move from a fixed annual withdrawal to a percentage-of-ending-portfolio-balance annual withdrawal.**

If the retirement account is governed by RMD rules, the only choice is whether or not the retiree invests their portfolio in a world of certainty (2% fixed return each year in this analysis) OR in a portfolio that will have variable returns (world of uncertainty). If the retiree chooses a 2% fixed return for their RMD-governed retirement portfolio, the outcome over the next 40 years will be astonishingly similar to having chosen a fixed withdrawal of $20,000 (4% of the starting retirement account balance). You can compare the figures in Column A and Column C to see for yourself. The only difference is that the portfolio governed by RMD rules still has a small remaining balance of $9,613 at the end of the 40th year.

Let's now turn our attention to the right-hand side of the "Retirement Income Menu"—the side that reflects a retirement portfolio that is invested in a diversified, multi-asset portfolio (a world of uncertainty). The results in this part of the analysis were derived from 1,500 iterations of a Monte Carlo simulation of portfolio returns that I designed. The average annualized 40-year return across the 1,500 simulations was 7.49% with a 40-year standard deviation of returns of 13.79%. The randomized portfolio had positive annual returns 66.2% of the time. These performance characteristics were specifically chosen to represent the type of volatility that we have observed in capital markets over the past 15-20 years. In a world of uncertainty (columns D-F) we observe that the retirement portfolio survived for at least 10 years 100% of the time (or in all 1,500 simulations). The average annual withdrawal during the first 10 years was highest if using the RMD guidelines ($26,753 in column F), but only slight higher than if withdrawing 4% of the portfolio balance each year ($26,136 in column E).

Table 2. Retirement Income Menu
Assuming a 4% Withdrawal Rate and $500,000 Starting Balance

$500,000 Retirement Portfolio 1,500 randomized simulations in the Variable Return Portfolio 40-Year Maximum Retirement Period	Fixed 2% Annual Portfolio Return			Variable Return Portfolio (based on 1,500 randomized simulations)		
	Fixed Annual Withdrawal of $20,000 No COLA (Withdrawal was 4% of starting balance)	Variable Annual Withdrawal Annual withdrawal of 4% of Year-End Portfolio Balance	Annual Withdrawal determined by RMD (starts at age 70.5)	Fixed Annual Withdrawal of $20,000 No COLA (Withdrawal was 4% of starting balance)	Variable Annual Withdrawal Annual withdrawal of 4% of Year-End Portfolio Balance	Annual Withdrawal determined by RMD (starts at age 70.5)
Column →	Column A	Column B	Column C	Column D	Column E	Column F
40-Year Annualized Return (%)	2.00	2.00	2.00	7.49	7.49	7.49
40-Year Standard Deviation (%)	0.00	0.00	0.00	13.79	13.79	13.79
Years with Positive Return (%)	100	100	100	66.2	66.2	66.2
Number of Years Portfolio Survived (40 max)	35	40+	40+	39.5 Ave	40+	40+
Least Number of Years Portfolio Survived	35	40+	40+	14	40+	40+
Portfolio survive 10 Years?	Yes	Yes	Yes	Yes	Yes	Yes
Total Amount Withdrawn in 10 Years ($)	200,000	185,927	196,304	200,000	261,357	267,535
Average Annual Withdrawal over 10 Years ($)	20,000	18,593	19,630	20,000	26,136	26,753
Portfolio Balance After 10 Years ($)	390,503	405,214	395,088	830,196	748,311	749,274
Portfolio survive 20 Years?	Yes	Yes	Yes	99.7% of time	Yes	Yes
Total Amount Withdrawn in 20 Years ($)	400,000	336,607	413,146	399,800	653,656	830,185
Average Annual Withdrawal over 20 Years ($)	20,000	16,830	20,657	19,990	32,683	41,509
Average Annual Withdrawal in Years 11-20 ($)	20,000	15,068	21,684	19,980	39,230	56,265
Portfolio Balance After 20 Years ($)	257,026	328,396	244,298	1,574,156	1,119,140	891,572
Portfolio survive 30 Years?	Yes	Yes	Yes	97% of time	Yes	Yes
Total Amount Withdrawn in 30 Years ($)	600,000	458,723	602,331	596,493	1,235,095	1,759,237
Average Annual Withdrawal over 30 Years ($)	20,000	15,291	20,078	19,883	41,170	58,641
Average Annual Withdrawal in Years 21-30 ($)	20,000	12,212	18,918	19,669	58,144	92,905
Portfolio Balance After 30 Years ($)	94,319	266,141	89,442	3,239,113	1,664,531	646,287
Portfolio survive 40 Years?	No	Yes	Yes	95.7% of time	Yes	Yes
Total Amount Withdrawn in 40 Years ($)	700,000 + 55	557,689	691,221	789,200	2,099,452	2,598,384
Average Annual Withdrawal over 40 Years ($)	20,000 for 35 yrs	13,942	17,281	19,730	52,486	64,960
Average Annual Withdrawal in Years 31-40 ($)	20,000 for first 5 yrs 0 for last 5 yrs	9,897	8,889	19,271	86,436	83,915
Portfolio Balance After 40 Years ($)	0	215,688	9,613	6,998,398	2,481,820	150,744

The retirement portfolio survived for 20 years 99.7% of the time if withdrawing a fixed amount of $20,000 each year (representing 4% of the portfolio's starting balance). In that same scenario, the average ending balance was $1,574,156 after 20 years—far larger than any of the withdrawal scenarios if the portfolio was earning a fixed 2% annual return. The fixed annual withdrawal portfolio survived the full 40 years in 95.7% of the simulations—with an average ending balance of just under $7 million. The average annual withdrawal over the full 40 years was $19,730 (or just slightly below the $20,000 figure which accounts for the rare cases when the portfolio was liquidated before the 40th year).

If, however, the annual withdrawal was variable (in this case 4% of the year-end balance each year) the portfolio lasted the full 40 years in every case (100% of the time). The average annual withdrawal over the 40-year period was $52,486 (see column E) and the average ending balance in the 40th year was just under $2.5 million. This approach gives the retiree more spending power compared to a fixed annual withdrawal of 4% of the starting balance ($20,000 annually in this case).

The RMD is clearly different—its job is to largely liquidate (and tax) the portfolio before the retiree is 110 years old. And it does that. But, it also guarantees the portfolio will not be empty prior to that age. The average annual withdrawal over the 40-year period was $64,960. But, it's worth noting that the RMD average withdrawal in the first 10 years (age 70-80) was $26,753—very close to the variable annual withdrawal of 4% of $26,136. Then, between the ages of 81-90 (years 11-20) the average annual RMD withdrawal was $56,265—far higher than any other amount in that same row of the table. Between the ages of 91-100 the average annual RMD withdrawal was $92,905. The next closest amount was $58,144. Those accelerated withdrawals using the RMD guidelines take their toll on the portfolio. By the end of the 40th year, the average ending balance in the RMD-governed portfolio was $150,744 compared to nearly $7 million in the fixed annual withdrawal approach and $2.48 million in the 4% of year-end portfolio balance withdrawal scenario.

In summary, for retirees that crave certainty they may want to consider a fixed return portfolio combined with a variable withdrawal (say, 4% of the portfolio balance each year) rather than a fixed annual withdrawal. The important distinction is that the variable annual withdrawal will result in **declining withdrawals from the portfolio each and every year** if the fixed return of the portfolio is lower than the withdrawal percentage (which was the case in this analysis). For example, the average annual withdrawal in column B between years 11-20 was $15,068 compared to $20,000 each year if using a fixed annual withdrawal. During years 21-30 the variable annual withdrawal drops to $12,212 while the fixed withdrawal stays at $20,000. The benefit in choosing a variable annual withdrawal (based on a percentage of the portfolio's value at the end of each year) is that you will still have money remaining after 40 years.

Conversely, if you choose a variable return retirement portfolio (such as in a broadly diversified, multi-asset class portfolio) AND want to maximize your retirement income (and have less remaining after 30 or 40 years) you will want to choose a variable annual withdrawal that is based on a percentage of the portfolio's value each rather than a fixed annual withdrawal. You will need to understand that the annual cash withdrawal that is based on a percentage of the portfolio's value each year can go down in some years. In other words, if the portfolio experiences a loss the annual cash withdrawal (say, 4% of the portfolio's value) will be reduced. While this may be frustrating, it is the exact mechanism that protects the portfolio from early failure.

So, to the question "will I run out of money?" the answer is generally no. At least, not for 40 years. The real key is how much money do you need each year? If withdrawing 4% of the portfolio balance will be sufficient, then a diversified, multi-asset variable return portfolio is very compelling. Settling for a lower, fixed return portfolio ignores the safety mechanism built into the math of a withdrawal system that only withdraws 4% of the portfolio's balance each year.

Technical Appendix B

Are You a Reluctant Investor?
By Craig L. Israelsen

Reprinted by permission from *Financial Planning Magazine*
https://www.financial-planning.com/search?query=israelsen

Perhaps you have been parked in cash for several years—maybe even many years (aka since 2008). You fear another decline in the US stock market—specifically in the equity markets of the world, but most notably in the US equity market. These fears are understandable as the last decline in the S&P 500 Index was in 2008—and that particular decline is extremely memorable in all the wrong ways.

As shown below in Table 1, since 2009 the large cap segment of the US stock market has produced nothing but positive annual returns. For a broader perspective, since 1970 the "batting average" of large cap US stock has been 81%--meaning positive returns in 81% of the calendar years. The past 10 years (2008-2017) the S&P 500 has produced positive returns 90% of the time—so we are in a positive streak that is above the 48-year average.

Small cap stock US stock has produced positive annual returns 71% of the time going back to 1970. Over the past 10 years, small cap US stock (as measured by the S&P Smallcap 600 Index) has produced positive annual returns 80% of the time—also higher than the historical norm.

Midcap US stock does not have a performance history back to 1970, but since 1992 (the past 26 years) it has produced positive annual returns 77% of the time. Over the past 10 years, midcap US stock has generated positive annual returns 70% of the time—so a bit under its longer-term average. However, two of those negative returns (-1.73% in 2011 and -2.18% in 2015) were trivial losses.

The point is simply this: many investors are likely anticipating a decline in equity markets—particularly the US stock market. The historical averages of positive and negative returns point to that. Their fears are also justified by the fact that average returns for US equity (large, mid, and small) over the **past 9 years (2009-2017) are each over 15%**--well above the longer-term averages of around 10+% for large and small cap and just under 12% for midcap (see Table 1). *As a result, you may be worried about investing now due to fear that the markets will tank sooner rather than later—and you want to avoid a "bad timing" experience.*

But, one cannot stay on the sideline hunkered down in cash forever—unless that person has a ton of money and is well into their 80s. At that point, they can be as conservative as they wish. For most everyone else we need to prudently invest for the future with a long-term perspective. Easier said than done when human emotions are involved.

One solution to the issue of "fear-of-bad-investment-timing" is to find an approach that is less sensitive to timing. This approach has two dimensions: **WHAT** you invest in and **HOW** you invest in it. (That being said, you may still choose to keep a portion of your assets in cash. What we are talking about now is the portion of your assets you choose to deploy back into non-cash investment assets such as US and non-US stocks, bonds, real estate, commodities, etc.).

Table 1. Past Decade for US Equity

Year	S&P 500 Index	S&P Midcap 400 Index	S&P Smallcap 600 Index
2008	-37.00	-36.23	-31.07
2009	26.46	37.38	25.57
2010	15.06	26.64	26.31
2011	2.11	-1.73	1.02
2012	16.00	17.88	16.33
2013	32.39	33.50	41.31
2014	13.69	9.77	5.75
2015	1.38	-2.18	-1.97
2016	11.96	20.74	26.56
2017	21.83	16.24	13.23
10-Year Average Annualized Return (2008-2017)	**8.50**	**9.97**	**10.43**
9-Year Average Annualized Return (2009-2017)	**15.25**	**16.83**	**16.37**

WHAT to Invest In?

Let's first talk about the **WHAT** to invest in. To dramatically simplify things I have chosen two different types of mutual funds (both happen to be Vanguard funds). One mutual fund represents the "market" as many investors refer to it—that is, a fund that mimics the S&P 500 Index. In this case, I am using Vanguard 500 Index (VFINX). Understandably, this fund is hardly a diversified approach to investing, but it does represent the type of fund that many investors think of when they contemplate getting "back into the market" (albeit the term "market" should, in fact, be reference to a wide variety of investment markets—but that is a pet peeve for another day). VFINX has 100% exposure to large cap US stocks, and uses a market capitalization weighted approach. It is, therefore, an investment in just one asset class—large cap US stock.

The other fund I have chosen is a fund-of-funds, specifically the Vanguard STAR fund (VGSTX). This particular fund invests in 11 other Vanguard funds and is diversified across several asset classes. Specifically, VGSTX has an allocation of roughly 40% to US equity (with roughly 80% allocated to large cap US stock and the balance allocated to midcap and small cap US stocks), 20% to non-US stocks, and 35% to bonds, and a small percentage in cash. In general terms, it employs a diversified 60% stock/40% fixed income approach.

As shown in Table 2 the ending outcome for each fund over the past 25 years is surprisingly similar. The 25-year average annualized return for VGSTX was 8.72% and 9.58% for VFINX. However, the path to those outcomes was very different—with VFINX being far more volatile (as noted by the higher standard deviation figures) and the significant losses in 2000, 2001, 2002, and 2008. This is an important issue inasmuch as it is precisely that type of volatility that may have caused you to pull out of equity investments in the first place—and having pulled out during periods of turbulence you would have likely failed to achieve either the 8.72% or the 9.58% return, but likely a return far below both of those.

Key observation: Vanguard STAR (VGSTX) generated 91% of the return of the large cap US equity market (as measured by VFINX) but with only 64% of the volatility. For skittish investors, that is an excellent tradeoff.

The results in the Table 2 below assume a lump sum investment of money at the start of 1993. In other words, the investor deposited a chunk of money on January 1, 1993 and never invested any more money over the entire 25-year period. By the way, this is the assumption behind all reported performance data.

Table 2. Two Funds, Two Approaches

25-Year Period	Moderate Risk 100% 60/40 Model Vanguard STAR Fund (VGSTX)	Aggressive 100% Large US Stock Vanguard 500 Index (VFINX)
1993	10.88	9.89
1994	(0.21)	1.18
1995	28.64	37.45
1996	16.11	22.88
1997	21.15	33.19
1998	12.38	28.62
1999	7.13	21.07
2000	10.96	(9.06)
2001	0.50	(12.02)
2002	(9.87)	(22.15)
2003	22.70	28.50
2004	11.60	10.74
2005	7.44	4.77
2006	11.65	15.64
2007	6.58	5.39
2008	(25.10)	(37.02)
2009	24.85	26.49
2010	11.70	14.91
2011	0.77	1.97
2012	13.79	15.82
2013	17.80	32.18
2014	7.35	13.51
2015	(0.15)	1.25
2016	6.55	11.82
2017	18.33	21.65
25-Year Lump Sum Return	8.72	9.58
25-Year Standard Deviation of Return	11.36	17.80
25-Year Internal Rate of Return of Annual Investments	8.60	9.48

HOW to Invest?

What if the investor (you) chose to "get off the sideline and back into the markets" gradually by investing money systematically over time rather than all-at-once upfront? This technique can reduce risk, specifically what we might refer to as "investment timing" risk which is very likely the concern that is keeping you on the sidelines and out of the investment markets.

Rather than re-entering the "market" all at once (i.e., a lump sum investment) the investor makes regular contributions (annually, quarterly, monthly, etc.) over a period of time. In fact, this is how most of us actually invest in 401k accounts, IRA accounts, etc. Shown in the last row of Table 2 is the internal rate of return (or IRR) when making annual investments into both funds over the past 25 years; 8.60% for Vanguard STAR and 9.48% for Vanguard 500 Index—both very similar to the 25-year lump sum returns. We now have our "benchmark" returns for both funds based on two methods of investing: **all-at-once** or **systematically over time**.

"Bad" Timing Scenario

Let's now evaluate a *bad timing scenario* in which the investor starts to invest on January 1, 2000—just before the US large equity market tanked for three consecutive years. This is a theoretical simulation of an investor who comes out of cash and re-enters the market(s) now in 2018—only to have the US equity market subsequently go into decline for several years.

We find in Table 3 the results of this sort of bad timing from a historical perspective, that is, starting an investment on January 1, 2000 and then experiencing 3 consecutive years of bad performance in large cap US equities (the fear of many on the sidelines right now). But wait, that only applies to VFINX which experienced losses of -9.06%, -12.02%, and -22.15%. Vanguard STAR had positive returns in 2000 and 2001, and a loss of just under 10% in 2002. Thus, it clearly matters WHAT we invest in. **For nervous investors (maybe YOU)— diversify, diversify, diversify. Vanguard STAR represents a much more diversified mutual fund than Vanguard 500 Index.**

Now, to the issue of HOW we invest. In this 18-year period from 2000-2017 a lump sum investment experienced the brunt of bad timing and finished with an 18-year annualized return of 5.29%. Vanguard STAR fared better with a return 6.96%. Interestingly, if the investor had chosen to invest money each year (say, $3,000) into each fund the internal rate of return (or IRR) for both funds was impressive: 8.41% for Vanguard STAR and 9.78% for Vanguard 500 Index. The idea of "bad" starting years doesn't apply to systematic investors who plan to stay invested for at least 10-15 years.

Moral of the story: systematic investing (annually, quarterly, or monthly) markedly reduces timing risk. Whereas lump sum investors are fully exposed to timing risk, investors that "get back into the markets" by making regular contributions (annually in this analysis) may actually benefit if markets decline during the first few years. And, if markets don't decline initially, that's OK too. Very simply, lump sum investors can only feel good initially if their investments have positive returns. Systematic investors can feel good either way—if performance is initially bad they are accumulating more shares with their subsequent investments. If performance is good, well...they can live with that.

So, if you are nervous about re-entering equity investments you might do so gradually. Kind of like marathon training. Don't start by running 26 miles.

Table 3. Bad Start
Investment started on January 1, 2000

18-Year Investment Period 2000-2017	Moderate Risk 100% 60/40 Model	Aggressive 100% Large US Stock
Bad Starting Years	Vanguard STAR Fund (VGSTX)	Vanguard 500 Index (VFINX)
2000	10.96	(9.06)
2001	0.50	(12.02)
2002	(9.87)	(22.15)
2003	22.70	28.50
2004	11.60	10.74
2005	7.44	4.77
2006	11.65	15.64
2007	6.58	5.39
2008	(25.10)	(37.02)
2009	24.85	26.49
2010	11.70	14.91
2011	0.77	1.97
2012	13.79	15.82
2013	17.80	32.18
2014	7.35	13.51
2015	(0.15)	1.25
2016	6.55	11.82
2017	18.33	21.65
Lump Sum Return 18-Year Period from 2000-2017	6.96	5.29
Annual Investing Return (IRR) 18-Year Period from 2000-2017	8.41	9.78

Technical Appendix C

Introduction to the *7Twelve*® Portfolio
By Craig L. Israelsen

This section introduces a multi-asset portfolio design that brings a higher standard to the notion of "diversified". This design is referred to as the *7Twelve*® portfolio. I designed the 7Twelve model in the spring of 2008.

The name "7Twelve" refers to "7" asset categories with "Twelve" underlying mutual funds. The seven asset categories are US stock, non-US stock, real estate, resources, US bonds, non-US bonds, and cash. The 7Twelve model is shown below in Figure 1.

The 12 mutual funds utilized in the 7Twelve design can be index funds, exchange traded funds (ETFs), or regular mutual funds. All 12 funds are equally weighted in the "core" 7Twelve model (each with an allocation of 8.33%). The equal-weighting is maintained by periodic rebalancing. There are also three "Age Based" versions of the 7Twelve model that progressively reduce the risk of the portfolio.

You can build the 7Twelve portfolio using mutual funds and/or ETFs from a variety of mutual fund companies.

Figure 1. The *7Twelve* Portfolio Model

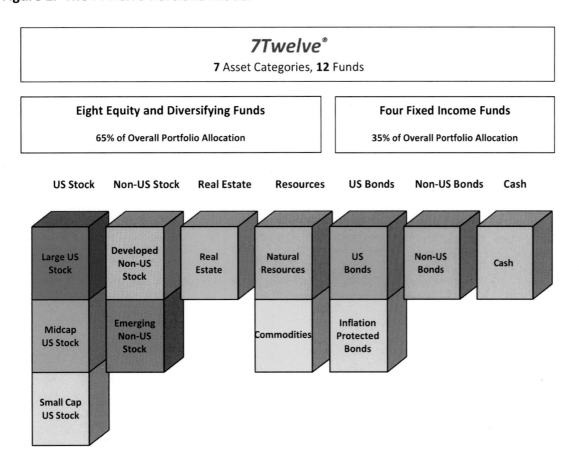

The performance of both the "active" and "passive" versions of the 7Twelve model over the past 20 years is shown in Table 1. Vanguard STAR (VGSTX) and Vanguard 500 Index (VFINX) are also included as comparison funds.

As shown below, the 7Twelve models (the Active 7Twelve that uses actively managed funds and the Passive 7Twelve that uses ETFs) outperformed both comparison funds over the past 20 years.

Table 1. 20-Year Performance of *7Twelve* vs. Comparison Funds (as of 12/31/2017)

Calendar Year Total % Return* (Assuming *annual* rebalancing)	Active 7Twelve (Using actively managed mutual funds)	Passive 7Twelve (Using passively managed ETFs)	Vanguard STAR (VGSTX)	Vanguard 500 Index (VFINX)
1998	0.39	1.54	12.38	28.62
1999	16.63	16.82	7.13	21.07
2000	11.21	5.42	10.96	(9.06)
2001	2.98	(1.94)	0.50	(12.02)
2002	2.18	(0.64)	(9.87)	(22.15)
2003	28.82	26.95	22.70	28.50
2004	19.79	17.80	11.60	10.74
2005	12.91	12.34	7.44	4.77
2006	15.98	14.96	11.65	15.64
2007	13.78	11.58	6.58	5.39
2008	(28.14)	(25.16)	(25.10)	(37.02)
2009	32.36	25.64	24.85	26.49
2010	14.52	14.41	11.70	14.91
2011	(6.31)	(1.00)	0.77	1.97
2012	12.42	10.64	13.79	15.82
2013	11.33	9.65	17.80	32.18
2014	0.05	2.50	7.35	13.51
2015	(6.96)	(5.07)	(0.15)	1.25
2016	9.19	10.14	6.55	11.82
2017	13.67	11.97	18.33	21.65
20-Year Average Annualized Return 1998-2017	**7.98**	**7.27**	**7.23**	**7.09**
20-Year Growth of $10,000	**46,476**	**40,714**	**40,402**	**39,372**
20-Year Standard Deviation of Annual Returns	**13.34**	**11.70**	**11.24**	**17.87**
Annual % Expense Ratio	**0.55**	**0.16**	**0.32**	**0.14**

20-Year Growth of $10,000
January 1, 1998 to December 31, 2017
(assuming **annual** rebalancing)

The core 7Twelve model equally weights all 12 asset classes (mutual funds) at 8.33% each as shown below. For those wanting to build one of the 7Twelve Age Based models the suggested allocations for each of the 12 asset classes are shown in Table 2 on the next page.

7Twelve® *Portfolio*

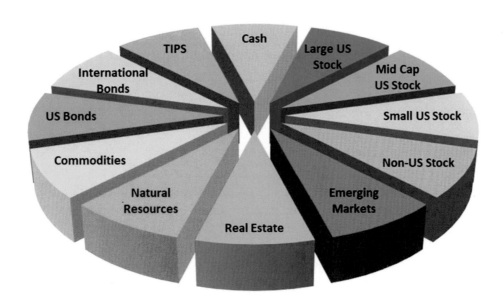

Table 2. Portfolio Allocations for the *7Twelve* Core Model and Age Based Models

7Twelve Model →	*7Twelve* Core Model	*7Twelve* Age Based 50-60	*7Twelve* Age Based 60-70	*7Twelve* Age Based 70 Plus
7Twelve Asset Category	*7Twelve* Age Based Portfolio Allocation			
Large US Stock	8.33%	6.67%	5.00%	3.33%
Mid Cap US Stock	8.33%	6.67%	5.00%	3.33%
Small US Stock	8.33%	6.67%	5.00%	3.33%
Non-US Stock	8.33%	6.67%	5.00%	3.33%
Emerging Markets	8.33%	6.67%	5.00%	3.33%
Real Estate	8.33%	6.67%	5.00%	3.33%
Natural Resources	8.33%	6.67%	5.00%	3.33%
Commodities	8.33%	6.67%	5.00%	3.33%
US Bonds	8.33%	6.67%	5.00%	3.33%
Inflation Protected Bonds	8.33%	6.67%	5.00%	3.33%
International Bonds	8.33%	6.67%	5.00%	3.33%
Cash	**8.33%**	**26.67%**	**45.00%**	**63.33%**

Rebalancing the *7Twelve* Portfolio

Rebalancing is a vitally important element of the 7Twelve design. Put simply, rebalancing is the process of systematically bringing each of the 12 funds in the 7Twelve portfolio back to their allotted allocation (8.33%) or, if you've built an age-based 7Twelve portfolio, back to the specified allocation (see Table 2). For example, sufficient money is taken out of the funds that performed better in the prior year and deposited into the funds that under-performed in the prior year to equalize the allocations across the funds. That's how simple rebalancing is.

There is empirical evidence to support the performance advantage of rebalancing. Over the 20-year period from 1998 to 2017, the Passive ETF-based 7Twelve with annual rebalancing produced an annualized return of 7.27%, compared to 6.86% without rebalancing—a benefit of 41 bps. That extra performance from rebalancing amounted to an extra $3,021 in account value after 20 years (assuming a $10,000 initial investment).

7Twelve as a Retirement Portfolio

The diversified 7Twelve portfolio performs well as an investment portfolio during the retirement years. The graph below illustrates the ending account balances on December 31, 2017 of a retirement account with a starting balance of $250,000 on January 1, 1998. The first-year annual withdrawal was 5% of the balance (or $12,500). The annual cash withdrawal was increased 3% each year over the 20-year withdrawal period amounting to a total withdrawal of $335,880. Two of the four Passive ETF 7Twelve models finished the 20-year period (1998-2017) with an ending balance greater than the starting balance of $250,000 (shown by the vertical dotted line). For comparison, the Active 7Twelve core model ended with a balance of $505,200 and Vanguard STAR finished with a balance of $321,043. The 7Twelve Portfolio has been a durable retirement model over the past 20 years, where the Active model outperformed the Passive model.

Retirement Portfolio Survival
20-Year Period
Ending Account Balance on December 31, 2017

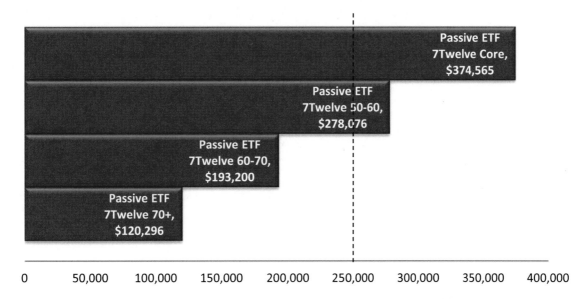

Building a diversified portfolio is only part of your game plan.
Set a goal to invest 10-15% of your income each year.

For more information about the *7Twelve*® Portfolio visit
www.7TwelvePortfolio.com

To read additional investing and portfolio design articles by Craig L. Israelsen
http://www.7twelveportfolio.com/Library.html
and
https://www.financial-planning.com/search?query=israelsen

To purchase current *7Twelve*® educational materials and portfolio construction guides
http://www.7twelveportfolio.com/Downloads/Web7TwelveReport.pdf

Questions? Email Craig at
craig@7TwelvePortfolio.com

Best wishes in the adventures ahead of you

Craig L. Israelsen, Ph.D., is an Executive-in-Residence in the Financial Planning Program at Utah Valley University (UVU) in Orem, Utah. Born in Palo Alto, California, he now resides in Springville, Utah with his wife Tammy. They enjoy church service, traveling to far-away places, and being close to children and grandchildren. Tammy devotes much of her spare time and energy to her children and grandchildren, family history research, and Days For Girls (https://www.daysforgirls.org/). They have seven children: Sara (Jon), Andrew (Shannon), Heidi, Mark (Kellie), Nathan, Emma, and Jared. They also have five wonderful grandchildren (three boys and two girls).

Dr. Israelsen holds a Ph.D. in Family Resource Management from Brigham Young University (BYU). He received a B.S. in Agribusiness and a M.S. in Agricultural Economics from Utah State University. Prior to teaching at UVU, he taught at BYU for 9 years and the University of Missouri-Columbia for 14 years.

Primary among Dr. Israelsen's research interests is the analysis of mutual funds and the design of investment portfolios. He writes monthly for *Financial Planning* magazine and is a regular contributor to Horsesmouth.com. His research has also been published in the *Journal of Financial Planning, Journal of Asset Management (U.K.), Journal of Performance Measurement, Asia Financial Planning Journal (Singapore), Journal of Family and Economic Issues,* and *Financial Counseling and Planning.*

His research has been cited in the Christian Science Monitor, Wall Street Journal, Newsweek, Forbes, Smart Money Magazine, Kiplinger Retirement Report, Advisor Perspectives, Dow Jones Market Watch, Family Circle Magazine, and Bottom Line Personal.

Dr. Israelsen is the developer of the *7Twelve*® Portfolio and the author of three books. Prior to this book, his most recent book is *7Twelve: A Diversified Investment Portfolio with a Plan* (John Wiley & Sons, 2010).

Hobbies include running, biking, swimming, woodworking, and family vacations. Dr. Israelsen has competed in the Boston Marathon five times...but has never won.

78359183R00020

Made in the USA
Middletown, DE
01 July 2018